Verses that mean a lot

'Coping with Illness and Grief'

CW00822207

Verses that mean a lot

For young people

'Growing up'
'Coping with Illness and Grief'
'Choice for Teenagers'

Books in preparation

For 4-8 years
'Being Young'

For Adults
'Daily Life'
'From Darkness to Light'
'A Different Journey'

Published by PLP Publishings, Buckingham, July 2007
PO Box 2150
Buckingham
MK18 1UR

Verses that mean a lot

'Coping with Illness and Grief'

by
Dr Audrey Coatesworth

Published by PLP Publishings, Buckingham, July 2007
ISBN 978-0-9555310-1-9

NOTE to the READER
This publication does not attempt to dispense or prescribe for or treat medical or psychological problems. If the reader - or other for whom this publication is intended, has significant difficulties in life it is highly recommended that they seek an appropriate health practitioner.

Printed and bound by Moreton Press, Buckingham

Ordering information

Tel/answerphone: 01280 823401
Websites: www.plppublishings.co.uk
www.plppublishings.moonfruit.com

PLP Publishings
PO Box 2150
Buckingham
MK18 1UR

Acknowledgements

Grateful thanks to:-

Peter – for devotion and love

Catherine - for patience and care

Brian and Nick - for invaluable help in the preparation of the books

The original pictures in the series were painted by
Yorkshire artist **David S Earnshaw**

Introduction

I trained at Edinburgh University Medical School and qualified as a Doctor in 1962. After my children started school and for the next thirty five years, until my recent retirement, I worked as a psychiatrist. I worked part time to fit in with school hours - against the tide or prejudice for women.

My psychiatric training was made possible by the insight and vision of one remarkable woman - Dr Rosemary Rue. She created the part-time womens' training scheme in the Oxford Region - recognizing the needs of both the married women doctors and their children.

My belief as a mother and grandmother, strengthened by my years of work, is that the safe and loving care of children is the greatest responsibility that anyone can undertake. I believe that as much time and effort, as is possible, should be given to this task - once chosen. Time that is missed cannot be regained – however important other aspects of life may appear at the time. Love, understanding, happiness or respect can not be bought.

But, with every possible care and love, we do not live in an ideal world. Death, absence, separation from and illness of someone we love, loss of a pet or personal illness cannot be avoided in life. For the grief section, I have included poems about death but also about transient situations where loss and sadness can be felt and where a child needs help and understanding to resolve their inner distress. Awareness of possible distress is important.

Some of the inspiration for the verses on illness came from my own childhood. My earliest years were during the anxious and 'deprived' days of the second world war – 'deprived' in the sense of the lack of the material possessions of the modern day child. But for me, the 'deprived' aspect of my childhood was the absence of effective medication. Thus, I had to live and cope with intermittent but severe respiratory problems without relief - other than the passage of time.

Living in the country, any medical advances of the time did not reach our doorstep. The only antibiotics that I remember were Penicillin lozenges for tonsillitis. There were no inhalers, no steroids, no nebulisers. Hot kaolin poultices or thermogene pads – placed on the chest – were used for respiratory infections! My grandmother lost five sons in childhood with the illness that I had – I survived, but was always aware that I, too, may not do so.

I have not attempted a comprehensive selection to cover all aspects of these topics. This is **not** a text book. I have written verses as they have come into my mind and from my heart – from the knowledge and understanding gained through life and work.

Understandings and experiences differ, so it is difficult to say precisely an 'age range'. As a guide, my intention has been that this book is suitable for young people, probably from 8 yrs upwards. Some of the poems may be understandable only in the teenage years, or need some discussion for younger readers. There is a choice of many in the book – some of which could fit into either the illness or grief section.

I would like them to be read by young people, but also **to** them - by parents and grandparents and by all those privileged to nurse, care for and teach sick or grieving young people.

The book is not just for those who are ill or grieving – but could give insight to those who are fortunate to have good health.

I hope these gentle verses will help anybody as and when they have to move through sad and difficult times and that adults as well as young people may also find hope or comfort for themselves in the verses.

Audrey Coatesworth
July 2007

CONTENTS FOR ILLNESS SECTION

CONTENTS FOR GRIEF SECTION

Poems
In
Times
Of

ILLNESS

A Bird

In times gone by, life was tough
For children who were ill
No medicines to make them well
Just days in bed, keeping still

§

Who are you? The child was asked
She thought – so hard she tried
'I know the name I'm given'
She said and then she cried
'I am a 'pet lamb' to my Daddy
I am 'naughty' to my Mum
A 'nuisance' to one brother
And I rarely have much fun
A bossy sister to another
A nursemaid to the third
But most of all I am ill
And I wish I was a bird

I would fly over the trees
To see what lies beyond
This quiet, little village which
Doesn't **even** have a pond
I think my world is really
A very small place to be
It could be better, I am sure, if
Something different I could see
But really I do nothing
My life is quite absurd
I just cough and wheeze daily

Yes

I wish I was a bird

A Child's Fears

The mother lay in her bed
She suffered a lot of pain
The little girl tiptoed in
Then tiptoed out again
'I cannot disturb her now
At last she is asleep'
She was only very young
Yet had a love so deep

'Can you make her better?'
She asked through all her tears

I will try my best for you'

It did not stop her fears
'What will happen if Mum dies?
I just pray that she gets better
Maybe, I can get some help

I will write to God a letter'

Dear God,

If you are there
We need help in this house
If my mummy can get well
I'll be quiet as a mouse
I will not make any noise
I'll clean up all my mess
I am hoping for an answer
Please, please can it be 'yes'?

A Long Night

I am awake, I have a pain
1 a.m. - that can't be right
I am tired, I need to sleep
That's the purpose of the night

2 a.m. - my eyes look round
The shadows seem to speak
'Why are you not asleep?
A good solution you should seek'

3 a.m. – time must have passed
So why is it not light?
I don't believe! Can it still be
The middle of the night?

4 a.m. - I'll make a drink
Milk, coffee, cup of tea
It doesn't really matter
Asleep I want to be

5 a.m. - just 3 hours left
Still a while to go
6 a.m. - now only two
Whatever shall I do?

I usually sleep like a baby
Or any koala bear
But I have had to spend
The night awake, it isn't fair

I hope no one annoys me
Or speaks in a loud voice
As my head will suffer
I just didn't have a choice

I may not be as pleasant
Excuses I shall not make
But if I should drop asleep
Just a short nap let me take

Please

A Mother's Love

I wept once, then I wept again
But my tears could not
Remove your pain

'Give me the hurt, dear God', I ask
But words come back
'It is not your task'

I would take each moment, all
I can only be there
If you should fall

A mother's love is not enough
Though I know for you
It is so tough

Together with you, pain I share
And in that doing
You know I care

Of my tears, you will see no sign
You have plenty
Without having mine

My anger - I will convert to strength
To stay and comfort
You at length

A Task

When I was born
The angels above
Were busy giving
The world their love
I think a novice
My list did pack
Health was forgotten
I couldn't go back
The difference to life
That would make
Was a stormy sea
Not a quiet lake
My boat survived
It did not sink
But it was harder
Than you'd think
No swimming in
A clear lagoon
Just avoiding rocks
With dangers strewn
So, if you are given
An important task
Just check the list
Don't fear to ask

Beautiful Places

I dream of a time
Pain has fled
I go for walks
Within my head
Down mountain paths
By forest lake
Beautiful places
I can make

I dream of sailing
Oceans blue
Seeing the world
In ship with crew
In sunny climes
I take a break
Beautiful places
I can make

I practise writing
Life in rhyme
So, in my bed
I waste no time
Despite pain
Make no mistake
Beautiful places
I can make

Being Forgotten

1.

I am told I'm not infectious
So tell me what I've got
What is it that makes me
Be alone, oh such a lot?
If it isn't very catching
Then why am I left here?
Does no one ever notice?
Or do they just not care?

2.

Did the doctor give instructions?
That I had to stay in bed
While everyone that I know
Gets up, goes out instead
I hear the others saying
'She is cold' or 'She is hot'
Somehow they don't see me
I'm alone, oh such a lot

3.

I don't know if they hate me
Or it's just they haven't time
I try to be so patient, and
I don't cry or even whine
Can someone please tell them?
I'm here. Have they forgotten?
I am still ill and in my room
I'm alone and feeling rotten

4.

I think I am really nice
And quite bright, you know
I can chatter and amuse
But alone, I feel so low
It isn't my choice to be ill
My body is not kind
But by myself I can at least
Learn to use my mind

5.

Maybe when I grow up
What I have learned will be
More valuable and important
Than all that school taught me
At least I'll know how to manage
If I'm ill, with no one there
Do you think that will help?
Because
Just now
My life isn't fair

7

Being Ill

I look out from my window, the trees have lost their leaves
Winter is here and I am stuck in bed, again, it seems
It can happen to me quite often, my life is passing by
I wish I was a kind of bird, as away from here I'd fly

I would go to New Zealand or Australia far away
Or find a desert island and there would pass my day
I would swim and gather food, I would lie upon the sand
I would bask in the sunshine - in a very different land

I wouldn't need any money or a roof above my head
I wouldn't need pop music, just to run around instead
There would be no infections, I would never have a pain
Only when it had gone from here, would I return again

I feel too ill to read a book or play with any toy
Or watch a TV programme, I am just a sick sad boy
My mum says I am brave, but I don't think that's right
As I cry a lot sometimes, alone, in bed - at night

When I get old, I shan't forget the difficult times I had
Living through awful days - when the pain was really bad
I shall try hard to get better, yes, as much as I ever can

Because

I want to grow up to be a big strong healthy man

'Bugs'

'I feel very ill, my tummy is sore
I cannot face food, don't give me more
I shall miss the fun, it won't be the same
I can do nothing, I can't play a game

Please make me well, I don't want to wait
Feeling so sick is something I hate
I may never fancy an ice-cream again
But I do not know what caused this pain

Make it go away, I am only small
I don't understand, why me at all?
Why can't you stop it? It is your task
To make me better is all that I ask'

*'I would do anything to stop you being ill
But that is something I cannot fulfil
That task is not in my loving power
But
I will take care of you - every hour*

*We will be happy when we hear your voice
As you play and dance and make lots of noise
Growing up can be sad or difficult or bad
We will do our best'*

'I'm better'

'I'm glad'

Caring Love

'For you I care
So I don't share
When I feel bad
I'd make you sad'

'To you I talk
I can not walk
But I am sad
If you feel bad'

'What I can do
Is to help you
I cannot share
Or your pain bear'

'Life is sad
But I am glad
That you are here
To wipe a tear'

'What I can do
Is be with you
Life isn't fair
But I will care'

'Illness is bad
It makes me sad
And spoils my days
In many ways'

'I love you
That's what I do
I'm always here
So - never fear'

Chicken-pox

I must have fallen into a nest of horrid stinging bees
This is what it feels like - will it never, ever ease?

I could not eat my breakfast or my dinner or my tea
The spots are in my mouth and sore as sore can be

They are in very awkward places - I cannot tell you where
It is somewhere never mentioned – but it is so hard to bear

I've been told that I have chicken-pox – **and** - it is quite bad
I have felt very ill for days, it makes me really sad

I want to scratch and scratch - the itch just drives me mad
Though it may sometimes help, the result can be quite bad

I don't want anyone to hear me - as swearing is not right
But **please** just tell me what to do when I try to sleep at night

'I think it should heal quite soon' - I heard the doctor say

I wonder

Will I still smile - when the spots have gone away?

Challenges to Face

'Why are you frightened, little girl'? I said
'I'm frightened of the pictures I see in my head
I am quite ill - and have not learned to cope
I have had so much pain, I have lost all my hope'

'Why are you crying, little girl'? I said
'I used to be happy, but I'm sad now - instead
Does anyone miss me - or hear when I call?
I cannot find comfort and I think I might fall'

'Please do not fear, little girl', I replied
'You are not weak, but strong - in your mind
You have climbed mountains - and you are not tall
You were very brave and you managed them all'

'Please do not cry, little girl', I said
'The sun will come out, put all clouds to bed
Then morning will bring its brightness and light
Your sadness will melt away with the night

Please understand, and listen - again
Our love for you could not stop the pain
Good times will come and you will get well
Your days will change, yes, that I can tell

Your smile gives your face a radiant glow
Not many people have your light to show
It would send away the darkest of shade
Your beauty shines – please - don't let that fade'

Chronic Asthma

I don't like to moan
When I cannot breathe
It's not my nature
What can I do
To get through?

I don't make a fuss
As I battle each day
I am quite brave
Should I shout?
To let it out?

I am quite desperate
I think I might cry
Will that make a difference?
Can any tears
Stop these fears?

Someone will notice
My awful distress
Is this child invisible?
They pass along
I must be strong

Minute follows minute
Nothing stops time
I will survive and live
I am sure
But for now -
I endure

Coping As Well As I Can

I can't believe this morning
Was part of the same day
If so, why hasn't this pain
Gone somewhere else to stay?
I have been very patient but
It was there when I saw light
It hasn't moved away at all
And now it's dark and night
I have counted all the flowers
On my papered bedroom wall
I have stayed still and quiet
And tried hard not to call
But, the pain drives me crazy
I don't know what to do
Please can you sit with me?
To help me to get through
They say it won't take long
And I will soon be 'right as rain'
I hope that by tomorrow I can
Say 'Goodbye' to pain
Sometimes I think that no one
Has ever had a pain like mine
But then I remember I had one
Before - and then was fine
So,
I just think about the words
My granny used to say

'Whatever happens, time will pass'

And

'Tomorrow is another day'

Daydreams

I like to think I am strong
I like to think I am brave
I like to think I could be
A person who could save
Someone from a burning house
Someone in a boat about to sink
Someone who was desperate
I just like to think

I would like to be quite strong
I would like to be quite brave
I would like to be someone
Who could another save
How can I be different?
When I am stuck in bed
I can be anything, anywhere
But only in my head

Someone said that I am strong
Someone said that I am brave
Someone said that I am kind
And I don't need to save
All I need is to carry on
With the courage I have so deep
That was really good to hear
So - those words I'll try to keep

Eczema

I scratch and scratch and still I scratch
My skin just drives me mad
One place first, then somewhere else
Never stopping - it is so bad
What can I do - please tell me?
To stop this itching? **NOW**
Before I scream and yell and shout
Help me, just tell me how

It wakes me when I'm fast asleep
The night becomes so long
I try hard not to make it bleed
But
Sometimes - I scratch too strong
It feels as though a host of ants
Lives - just beneath my skin
Or tiny people with nettle leaves
Run round - this itch to bring

But getting it all to go away
Is not possible, though I ask
Please, please can someone help me?
Give me another, easier task
I am praying that one day soon
I shall have some peace
The itching will stop and the war
With all my skin will cease

You will see a smile on my face
As I no longer wish to hide
I will look quite normal
And walk around with pride
When my skin is pink and clean
You will see the real me
I am inside this awful mess

Waiting

I wonder

Will that time ever be?

Encouragement Forgotten

Do I ever hear - 'well done'?
Two other words to find
'Never mind'
I will not be upset
You mean to be quite kind

Maybe my highest mountain
<u>Is</u> just a little hill
'Never mind'
Yes, it only seems big
Because I have been ill

Maybe my deepest ocean
<u>Is </u>a splash upon the way
'Never mind'
Yes, I must remember
There will be another day

Another day of struggling
Another day to fight
But - **you** 'never mind'
Because one day

Yes

I am going to be alright

Having A Pain

Have I been naughty? Have I been bad?
Have I done wrong? Is it something I had?
Am I to blame for having this pain?
Can I go away, and come back again?

Could I return and start back as new?
I would if I could - if only I knew
Would I start with my hands or with my head?
Or with my feet and body instead?

Go away pain and never come back
I would like to fasten you in a big sack
In the dustbin, quick, I would throw
I do not like you, go away now, go

I have to stay here, I cannot change
But over the whole world you can range
Nobody likes you, that you can learn
You just bring misery wherever you turn

But - don't find another small boy or girl
Just disappear in a big, darkened swirl
Go high into the sky, go ever so high
Please don't come back, no - don't even try

Influenza

I can **not** get up today
If you insist I shall create
I can **not** put on my clothes
And my teeth will have to wait

I can **not** get out of bed
As my legs have no lift
It feels as if all my brain
In sleep just wants to drift

I can **not** be bothered
With anything or anyone
My head is really hurting
I don't feel like having fun

I am **not** being lazy
This is horrid, not my choice
I just need to be quiet
So, please don't make a noise

Go away, leave me alone
Till another, different day
And when I can feel better
I'll get up -
                    and go and play

Invisible Chains

There are no chains to bind me
No lock on bolted door
Yet I cannot move with ease
Nor freely wander o'er
The hills, or far off valleys
Green fields or pastures new
My room is like a prison
I have no other view

Bound by illness, long and dire
Limited beyond employ
For walking, or for roaming
Life to live, not to enjoy
Year upon endless year
Shall I still this battle win?
When my breath is released
My heart will surely sing

Just For Me

I want to write a happy poem
A poem to make me smile
To put with letters to myself
In my special mementoes file

I have tried and tried all day
But the words I cannot fake
I really want to be happy
Is that such a big mistake?

How do I write a funny poem?
One that makes me laugh
When I am always stuck in bed
With a tight and wheezy cough

Maybe I should write my poem
About playing in a park
Another day will soon be gone
It's already getting dark

It's been quite a busy day
Just thinking what to say
But it has seemed very hard
As the words all go away

So I will try to go to sleep
As my poem I cannot write
I really hurt too much to laugh
While coughing through the night

I will try again tomorrow
Yes, that **is** my latest plan
I want to write a happy poem
For me -
　　　my biggest fan

Keep Going

I'm invited to a party
Excited as can be
I get dressed up
In my head
But on the day
I'm ill in bed

I'm going on a holiday
Excited as can be
I pack my clothes
In my head
But on the day
Stay home instead

I'm going to a concert
Excited as can be
Travel the journey
In my head
But on the day----

Enough said

I still plan activities
Excited as can be
To different places
In my head
I keep going

As by **hope**

I am still led

Learning To Accept

I heard a story of a tortoise
Who tried to race a hare
The tortoise won in the end
And the hare tried not to care

I live that race every day
As my mind is like the hare
My ill body is the tortoise
And **I** don't think it's fair

Make the tortoise think as the hare
And put the hare inside a shell
I wonder what kind of story
Both of them would tell?

Is this what life is all about?
Little choice, but do our best?
To accept the road is difficult?
Life is different from the rest?

But

It **could** be much, much worse
Look around and you will see
The tortoise who cracked it's shell
A hare as dull as dull can be

Better to be me than that bully
Who can think or run any race
One day when he meets his maker
He will have egg on **his** ugly face

So - I accept that I am me
And - **I** now understand
That life is not about any race

But

Holding out a helping hand

Life Style

'Can I breathe as I awake?'
That is my first question
Not – 'What should I wear?'
But - 'Can I get any air?'

Blue, pink, yellow, green
Trousers, skirt or dress?
It matters not till I know
What for me the day will show

'Shall I go out shopping?'
or
'Arrange to meet a friend?'
I cannot decide for a while
'Can I, today, walk half a mile?'

Always, every day the same
Restricted by a system
Ideas not allowed to flow
First of all - **I must know**

'Will I ever be free to have
Questions like the others?
Shall I ever my life share
With no pain

But

Lots of air?'

Little Girl

Little girl you are so sweet
Like a cake too good to eat
Little girl you are so bright
Like a strong and shining light
Little girl you are so brave
Like a lion in its cave
Little girl you are such fun
Like a day - warm with sun
Little girl you cope so well
When you have pain - I can tell
Little girl you can be tough
Like an anchor if it's rough
Little girl, 'courage' is your name
Like a terrier, you are the same
Little girl you are so kind
Like a whisper in my mind
Little girl, you are so strong
Even though each hour is long
Little girl, you make me proud
Lighting up a big black cloud

Little girl, I'm trying to say
I love you dearly, every day

Living With Eczema

I scratch all night, I scratch all day
But still the itch won't go away
It drives me mad - it just goes on
Until another day is gone
It is painful, sore and red
I want it pale and cool instead

I dream that I am like a snake
And a brand new coat I make
Old one take off, and throw it down
And I dress in a smooth silk gown
In pink and cream - so soft to feel
Then I leave my skin to heal

Ointment's smell is put away
A flower crown for me today
Like a princess I shall be
A beautiful face for all to see
Not scarred by nails while I'm asleep
No one, again, a watch must keep

But the dream soon fades away
As I have to meet another day
I must accept and learn to know
My beauty from inside must show
I did not ask this skin for me

Please -
>   **Judge me not** by what you see

Love

Can you imagine a big big cloud?
That is made of lots of love
It floats over roof tops
In the sky high up above

It's a cloud for little children
In all parts of the world
A cloud when they are hurting
And their cries are never heard

Its rain brings tears of comfort
Sent from angels in the sky
Giving love to every child
Not something you can buy

Some children are alone and sad
Their hurt is there to stay
Are you one of the lucky ones
With love at home each day?

Maybe Tomorrow

1.
Maybe tomorrow
I shall be well
Did someone come
And cast the spell
At my birth
My first day here?
So I became ill
And carried fear?

2.
Maybe tomorrow
I'll understand
Why I am where
I must stand
I wasn't told
They didn't ask
I was simply given
Ill health - my task

3.
Maybe tomorrow
I'll have strength
To decide my path
The width and length
Instead of chains
Around me fast
Pain disappears
Into the past

4.
Maybe tomorrow
I shall be free
To walk and talk
Fresh things to see
To travel around
Where and how
I want to be there
I can't - just now

5.
Maybe tomorrow
I shall be told

' Your chains fall off
They rust, are old'

I shall be me
Free at last

'**Keep hope**, *my friend*
And hold it fast'

Mild Delirium

I have lost my way
In a haze
This place of shadows
Like a maze

Monsters creep
All about
I am trapped here
Can't get out

Who can help?
No one around
Where is the path?
Stony ground

This is frightening
And I shake
A light appears
Then I awake

Bad dream has gone
I tremble still
Why did it happen?

'You were ill'

Missing Out

Watching from the sidelines
Hearing others play
I want to join in with them
Not stay in bed all day
Nor wait, because I cannot run
Stay at home, not go to school
When I return I never know
What to do, what is the rule

Where is everything I missed?
In cupboard - blue or red?
Which book should I read?
I don't know, no one has said
I ask, but others do not show
I look, but search in vain
What things have been learned?
Such a puzzle, such a strain

Then - just as I understand
At least - that's what I think
I am ill, I cannot breath
And I feel my sad heart sink
Everything begins again
Bed, pain, no school, no friend
Just missing out on everything
So - I must just pretend

I want to be well and happy
Not live days within my head
There isn't a lot that comes true
If you spend your time in bed
One day in the future
When I'm able to play and run
I shall get the most from life
And make sure I have some fun

My Way

I keep on believing
That soon it will be light
I update my prediction
Each hour of the night
Coping with a dark minute
That follows the one before
How I long to get free
And run out of the door
Run away from darkness
Climb a rainbow on the way
Travel the world on a star
In some orbit I would stay
Until I can breath freely
Dread vanished into space
And it is time for me to have
Peace - in my own place
Sleep quietly in my own bed
Be able to run and play
I keep on believing
It will happen to me one day

Never Beaten

I cannot breath
I cannot move
I cannot eat
Not my will
I am ill

I want to play
I want to skip
I want to run
Up the hill
I am ill

Stop the world
Turn time back
To a time
It was my will
I was not ill

Nuisance me
Needs to meet
Making work
Others to fill
I am ill

Look ahead
See some light
Fight the pain
Wait until
I am not ill

Understand
Another's pain
Learned within
'Through the mill'
When I was ill

Normal Reaction

I am a sad person
To be happy I try
People ignore me
I don't know why
I will help anyone
I am quite kind
I give my time
And I do not mind
What makes me sad?
Well
I fell down one day
Those who saw me
Just turned away
They didn't give back
Any bit that I gave
Instead walked past
Not even a wave

I am a sad person
Do you understand?
As no one noticed
I needed a hand
I used to be happy
Before I was ill
I was liked then
As needs I could fill
But
Once I was empty
My task was done
No one gave thought
I needed some fun
Support and comfort
Time and a place
At any table I need
Just a very small space

Nothing

No one answers
No point to ask
To endure
Is my task
No relief
Can be sought
I continue and
Ask for nought
Disappointment
Is the fate
If I should hope
Or think to wait
Accept the truth
Fun is around
But lost for me
It can't be found
Pain takes joy
In its wake
Spoils all effort
That I make
So now I never
Expect to see
Any pleasure
Just for me
To conquer pain
Win the fight
When the day
Has turned to night
Light is dim
Pains filter grey
I must accept

(For now)

It is this way

Not My Choice

Being ill has made me see
That I did not ask to be me
Life is meant to be a gift
Did I the wrong parcel lift?
One that held a lot of pain
I will **never** do that again

Will I ever get the chance
To play and sing or even dance?
Visit a place I haven't been
Hidden all this time, unseen?
Whatever else - I must endure
I found **courage** - that is sure

I know that I am quite **strong**
So not everything was wrong
I have **patience**, I feel l**ove**
They were given from above
So, I accept I came as me
I have **hope**, and I am free

Painful Days

Will I wake up one rainy day
Still to know this pain will stay?
Another day and maybe more
No way out of that closed door
Friends in imagination play
At least I 'see' those every day
We have fun when my eyes close
I block out all, then, have a doze
I awake to find nothing new
I just have to live this through

Will I wake up one sunny day
Find this pain has gone away?
Will I run or will I walk?
Will I shout or will I talk?
Will I play or will I fight?
Will I sing and get it right?
So many things I want to try
And I just know I will not cry

No

Never again will my tears fall

'Why'?

Because

I have already cried them all

Perseverance

I'm going to have a few days holiday by the sea
With people that I love, and I am full of glee
I've packed my case - with special clothes to take
And now - there is only the journey left to make

**Oh no, I don't believe it - it really can't be true
I can't go, I am ill - whatever shall I do?**

A birthday party has been arranged, I have been invited
I can't wait for tomorrow, I really am excited
A lovely tea and some games, I shall be with all my friends
We shall have a lovely time – and be sorry when it ends

**Oh no, I don't believe it - it really can't be true
It can't happen, I am ill - whatever shall I do?**

A dance troupe has come to town – the tickets have been paid
It is sure to make a memory, that will never, ever fade
I can almost feel the energy, the excitement of the dance
I can't wait to see them – it's my one and only chance

**Oh no, I don't believe it - it really can't be true
I shall miss it, I am ill - whatever shall I do?**

Should I try, I wonder, to arrange something new?
Or should I just remember what can happen when I do
Looking forward is exciting, disappointment makes me sad
But
I am quite determined to do things that make me glad

I don't quite believe it – but it really can be true

I went

I was there

I hope it's the same for you

Private Wishes

So that I can keep my hopes
I have my private wishes
In my head, through each day
I put ideas in coloured dishes
Blue – for when I am quite well
And I am free to roam
In green or yellow I prepare
For when I'm ill – in bed - at home

I may plan to knit a jumper
Or to read a favourite book
Maybe on the television
Is a film - that's worth a look
But sometimes I'm too tired
So I must just stay in bed
And then I make more wishes
Until they fill my head

Do you think I'm being silly
When I tell you what I do?
But no one ever tells me
A better way to get me through
On the days when I have pain
And I don't have any choice
I just talk about my wishes
With my inner private voice

Puzzle Pain

I have a pain
The worst I had
I don't know if
I'm good or bad

He was bad
He had a pain
And no one knew
He broke my train

She was good
She had a pain
She washed the dishes
Put them to drain

So why have I
Got this bad pain?
I have done nothing
Can you explain?

If good has pain
And bad has pain
Being bad or good
Has nothing to gain

'Good or bad
I will make it plain
Has seldom to do
With having a pain'

Solitaire

'I just play Solitaire
For hours and hours on end'

'What a brilliant way to cope'

'No, it seems a waste to spend
Hours and hours of my life
Just distracting from the pain
Struggling to even breathe
Until some ease I gain

I want to be free to do
Whatever I choose or want
To travel, to work, or to play
And someone that wish to grant
Here, I do not want to be
It really is not fair
To have to stay in bed all day
And just play Solitaire'

You wouldn't like it either

Someone To Care

The porcupine has got spines
The hedgehog prickles too
The snail can hide inside its shell
What can a small child do?

The tiger has got massive teeth
The wasp a nasty sting
The lion has enormous strength
What did the small child bring?

The antelope can run with speed
The birds can fly so high
The whale can dive so very deep
What can the small child try?

Intelligence is not enough
Being good can be in vain
Helplessness may be ignored
A hurt child cries in pain

What protection did she bring?
As nothing could she carry
Dependent on those around
Till old enough to marry

Love should be her blanket
From deep within the heart
Of those who had decided
In their life she played a part

Then no tiger's teeth could bite
No wasp or bee would sting
A small child needs protection
So the heart can learn to sing

The Fairy's Gift

The gift was wrapped in paper
Carried in her outstretched hand
'This is for you, please accept it'
The fairy said, with a wave of her wand

'What is in that gift so fine?'
'The fairy King from his palace grand
Has sent it, special delivery
I must give it to your own hand'

Bemused, the gift she opened
Her eyes were amazed to see
Within a glass casket on velvet
'Why, that book was written for me'

The book had a cover of white satin
Her name she saw, printed in bold
'The story of your life is here
Past and future you are told'

She woke and she was all alone
Her chest hurt from coughing dire
Her breathing was still difficult
She had feared she would expire

The dream stayed as some dreams do
It was kept in a special place
She remembered it in times of need
Hope - given by the hand of Grace

The Ice-Princess

The ice-princess came to see me
'Really? Who is she?'
She is dressed all in white
And she softly spoke to me

She wore a sparkling tiara
'Really? What did she say?'
She said that I was special
And I would be well one day

She carried a very big white bag
'Really? What was it for?'
To carry my anger and sadness
I don't need them any more

She takes hurt and pain away
'Really? Where will it go?'
To the bottom of the sea -
Well, actually, I don't know

She asked what I would like to do
'Really? What did you say?'
I said it would be wonderful
To be able to run and play

I wondered why I was chosen
'Really? Did you ask?'
Yes, but she just listened
While she went about her task

I asked her where she came from
'Really? Did she let you know?'
From far away in a beautiful place
Where all good people go

I said 'Thank you kind ice-princess'
'Really? What was her reply?'
She said it was her pleasure and
My courage made her cry

The Keyhole

In front of me the door is locked
Through the keyhole I see a park
Flowers bloom, the colours shine
But I am here, still in the dark

'You've a key, please let me use it
To open that door, be free
Why are you in here with me?
When you could sit by yonder tree?'

In the shade, by the flowing stream
I can see others, at play, today
Yesterday and the days before
Behind the door I have to stay

'Give me the key please, I beg
Let us go out from this dark place
Into the light and sunshine warm
Get some colour in my pale face'

'My key is not the key
For the door that binds this space
It belongs to another time
And to a very different place

I am here, you are not alone
When the door can open wide
You will walk out proudly
Breathe the warm fresh air outside

Illness has long imprisoned you
But if you manage to get free
Use the courage you needed here
And you'll be as strong as any tree'

The Need To Dream

I dream I shall be able
To live as others do
Days will be like summer
Smiles a whole day through
No pain to spoil each hour
No effort to walk or run
To holiday in far off places
I mean to have some fun

Is it wrong for me to want
A share in carefree days?
It's been so long, I must try
To remember different ways
How to get up early
Race around and get things done
Without the constant struggle
Then this battle will be won

It is not all wasted effort
To plan and hope this way
I have learned to look forward
And meet another day
Endurance can be practised
Through winter snow and frost
Keep hoping - it is the only way

Give up dreams?

You must be joking

If I do - I may get lost

The Search

One day I shall leave my childhood well behind
I shall do what I want, and happiness I'll find
Health is like a jewel, something took it all away
I must search for it, I will, I know, soon, one day

I shall look everywhere, I shall try, until I find
I just need help - from some people who are kind
I do not know its colour, I do not know its size
I do not know where it is, but I will find that prize

Somewhere it is waiting, I just have to struggle on
I shall know I've found it, when my pain has gone
I shall do lots of things, go right around the world
See many people and make sure **my** voice is heard

I shall leave this little room, full of pain and tears
Out of the door I will go, and leave behind my fears
Black clouds will disappear, I shall see my future bright

I keep all these thoughts, to help me through the night

Then, no one will take me where I don't want to go
No one will leave me with people I don't know
No one will hurt me, or push or thump or hit
No one will frighten me again
                           No
                          Not one tiny little bit

Things That Cannot Be Bought

I saw a man, he had a coat, like gold it shone so clear
I asked him where he bought it, and had it cost him dear?
'You cannot buy a coat like this', he replied to me
'It is called **Courage**, but it did not come free
I went through a field of pain, I got to the other side
I had no one to help me and no horse with me to ride'

I saw a man wearing a hat, it was like a silver moon
I asked him where he bought it, and could I get one soon?
'You cannot buy a hat like this', he replied to me
It is called **Kindness**, and it did not come free
I helped one who was lost, and one who could not walk
One who had no food and drink, and one too ill to talk

I saw a man with shiny boots, strong, light - as if a feather
I asked him where he bought them, he said he hadn't - ever
'You cannot buy boots like these', he replied to me
They are called **Endurance**, and they do not come free
I had to work beyond my strength, and for so very long
No other there to lift the load, and no help came along

I saw a man with a light, that shone so far and bright
I asked him where he bought it, as it beamed into the night
'You cannot buy a light like this', he replied to me
It is called eternal **Hope**, it was given to me - free
I had lost direction, I had battled to the end
I had coped when all was lost, for myself I had to fend

Then a light I suddenly saw, upon my darkest day
I did not ask, it was just there, and then I found my way

You have to find your **Courage**
Kindness comes from very deep
Endurance needs much effort
but
Hope is yours - to keep

Thoughts

1.
The little child lay awake
Another awful day to face
She would rather be anywhere
But in this dreary place

2.
She looked through the window
Gazed at a sky already blue
And thought of many lovely things
She would like to make come true

3.
She kept herself busy
Making pictures in her head
Of what she would like to do
If she was up and well – instead

4.
A career would be very nice
A husband and children too
But first she had to 'grow up'
The hardest thing she had to do

5.
As she was often very ill
For months without a break
Life was difficult, she was sad
Much pain she had to take

6.
She could not have a picnic
Her bed would fill with crumbs
She had no one to talk to
So, just twiddled her two thumbs

7.
A thought caused fear within her
'Will anyone remember me?
At school or in the village
Will they know it's me they see?'

8.
So many lessons missed at school
To find what had been learned
She had tried before, and only
Confusion had been earned

9.
'I am like a pale chrysalis
My life lived in a shroud
But when my butterfly wings open
I shall fly from this dark cloud'

10.
So, she used her imagination
To help through each dark day
She 'grew up' and her pictures
Became her future

That - truthfully

I can say

Thoughts At Bedtime

Please let me sleep this night
Free from pain and fear
Let me know the comfort
That you are always near
Holding me by my right hand
Listening for my needy call
Helping me to rest a while
Making sure that I don't fall
What shall I do, I wonder?
When shall I be strong?
Will the night pass quickly?
Or the hours seem very long?
Please let me sleep this night
Free from pain and fear
Let me feel your presence
And know that you are here

Told - 'As It Is'

'Do you have a dog? Do you have a cat?'
'No, I have nothing, no, nothing like that
My life is listening for the big clock to chime
Counting the hours and minutes of time'

'Do you travel on holiday to places of fun?
Bathe in the sea and bask in the sun?'
'No, I go nowhere, I just lay in my bed
Thinking about that, but just in my head'

'Have you some friends who visit each day?
Who bring you books and on the lawn play?'
'No, no one comes calling, I do not play out
I just want to scream. I try hard not to shout'

'Do you go to the pictures, watch TV and sing?
See new lambs dancing in fields every spring?'
'Your teasing is hurtful, please do not speak
I can do without you and no comments I seek

If you cannot help, I'd prefer you to leave
I can carry on learning my own belief
That one day in the future, I shall be well
I shall write many books as my stories I tell

In my mind I go places you'll never know
And travel through time, that I will show
I know things, through illness, that others can't see
Though it's been very hard, I am glad I am me'

Walking Forward

I walk on rough mountain tracks
Up hills to tarn and dale
Along the flowing riverside
Midst bluebells and wooded vale
Swim in warm sea, bask in the sun
Play tennis in the shade
This is what life is meant to be
For simple pleasures I was made

I have no wish to drink, take drugs
Spend my nights in smoky clubs
These things offer nought to me
I find no place in crowded pubs
The peace and quiet, the vistas
From a hillside, high and wide
To hear the birds, see wild flowers
Free to breathe fresh air - outside

But all that is only in my mind
From imagination rich and true
Helping me get through each day
Until I do these things with you
I **will** walk and I **will** run
Over open mountain track
When I am well, I know I shall

Waste no time looking back

Weariness

Weariness like a big strong arm
Enfolds me in its grasp
I couldn't walk another mile
Or run from any wasp
It binds my legs in strong twine
My arms are weights of lead
And really - I will not mention
The bad ache within my head
Somehow it soaks into my bones
Takes enthusiasm all away
My goals are lost within the mist
I can't look forward to the day
What can I do to fight it?
It's dreadful, awful, dire
I have to do something quickly
Otherwise I may expire
A healthy meal just doesn't help
Sleep never is enough
Will it ever disappear?
Life is so very tough

Yes

The light bulb will be on again
The tyres be filled with air
The tank will be refuelled
The barometer will read 'fair'.
Then the days will seem short
As feet spring along the road
My movements will be light as air
When I shed this heavy load
I shall dance and I shall sing
Enjoy the wind and sun
And one day, in the future
I shall have some well earned fun

What To Do

'I don't know what to do'
I hear a small voice say
'I am stuck and I don't like
Where I have to stay

I don't know what to do
There's no one I can meet
It's not like me, but really
I feel too ill to greet

I don't know what to do
There is the open door
But I cannot reach it
I can't walk any more

I don't know what to do
Or find the way to go
I want to see the sun and
Feel the winds that blow

I don't know what to do
Please tell me how to be
So that I can understand
It's alright to be me'

Poems
In
Times
Of

GRIEF

Absent Friend

I wonder 'Why had you to die?'
You were always very kind
The best friend I ever had
I may not another find
You liked the same things as me
And laughed at what I said
Now you are gone and I am left
With just memories in my head

I wonder 'Where have you gone?'
Is heaven in light or dark?
Can you walk, go for a swim?
Or play in any park?
I wish I knew the answers
Then I wouldn't be so sad
If I know that you are happy
I would try to be quite glad

I wonder 'Shall I see you again?'
When I die and I am old?
Or will you have moved somewhere?
Heaven's very big, I'm told
I shall always remember you
And be pleased you were my friend
But, it really is so unfair
That your time with me should end

I wonder ' Will you remember me?'
Will you grow up or stay the same?
Have you photographs in heaven?
Will you have another name?
I have so many questions
They are mostly in my head
If I ask - I may seem silly
So, I just sit and think - instead

A Child's Sadness

I am sad, so very sad
More sad than I can say
I want to run about
To sing, to dance, to play
But I cannot
So I am sad, so very sad
More sad than I can say
I want to smile and to laugh
And wipe the tears away
But I cannot
So I am sad, so very sad
But more I cannot say

A Grieving Child

The tears are like falling rain
The sun is hidden above
A dark cloud, that covers
A child who feels no love

The face shows staring eyes
Searching amidst the gloom
Listening for absent footsteps
A child feels only doom

Walking through the fog ahead
The path seems dark and long
Trying to get through each day
A child has to be strong

The wind blows in the trees
Biting sharp and cold
Will the sun shine again?
Before a child grows old

Alone, the way is not found
Lost in the dark of grief
Another must bring some light
Then a child can find relief

A gentle hand is needed
To hold the days together
When the raging storm has passed
A child greets fairer weather

A Message

I see the sun, the flowers, the trees
Other children out at play
But I cannot join in the fun
I'm feeling bad
Alone and sad

One day I shall be grown up
Remember how it was
That I was really very brave
And time still passes on
With no song

For children living in the dark
This message is just for you
Keep a torch within your mind
Awful moments will pass by
You can cry

If the saddest path you tread
Understand and be quite sure
Endurance will your lesson be
Learned by you loud and clear
With a tear

I know that children cannot choose
The lives that they must live
But we can all try to be kind
Believe in goodness, not in hate
A better fate

Broken Promises

'Where have they gone?'
The little girl said
From her hospital bed that night
I see faces - but none I know
This cannot be quite right
The fear rose in her stomach
She was angry with them all
'What will happen? I shall cry'
But still no tears did fall

'Where has she gone?'
The little girl said
When she went to school that day
She hadn't been left there before
She didn't know she had to stay
The fear rose in her stomach
She was angry with them all
'What will happen? I shall cry'
But still no tears did fall

'Where do I go?'
The little girl said
Turned off the bus that day
Her money had been stolen
At the bus stop she had to stay
The fear rose in her stomach
She was angry with them all
'What will happen? I shall cry'
But still no tears did fall

'When I grow up',
The little girl said
'And look after my own child
I promise I shall never leave
I shall watch and try to guide'
The fear rose in her stomach
She was angry with them all
That promise - she had to break
Then her tears did fall

Child Alone

I listen but no one talks
I search but no one walks
I can see, it seems like night
I look around, no one in sight
I will climb high, I am not tall
No one there, big or small
Round the corner I will look
Are all kind people in a book?

Why does no one notice me?
Have I no form that they can see?
Maybe I'm not here at all
No one hears my voice so small
The sound must quickly disappear
Or surely someone would appear
I must be like a little ghost
But I am very scared - the most

I hurt and some comfort need
To ease my pain, please give heed
It's everywhere, if you should ask
Has not someone got that task?
I can then go back to sleep
Arms round my teddy I will keep
Why must I stay in this place?
I do not know another face

I just hope that one day soon
I will wake up on the moon
I will ride on sunbeams warm
And sit on stars above the storm
Nothing will ever hurt me there
I wouldn't have to say a prayer
But I believe no one would care
They'd only miss my teddy bear

Childhood Days

(The 'ogre' of parental mental illness)

The boy stood at the railings, his young fresh face alight
Freedom now, as all was well, but would it last another night?
Or would the ogre again appear, change one he knew should care
Into a beast with cruel tongue, who tore things - beyond repair

The sea stretched out behind him, a boat waited, waves to ride
'One day I will take that journey, and no longer want to hide'
Unpredictable were his childhood days - passing with the cloud
Caused by the mother's illness, no happiness was allowed

Anger and sadness bottled up. Why must it be this way?
'I wish the ogre would disappear. I don't want it to stay'
But for all his love and kindness, he never had a choice
The ogre of illness beat her, and altered her sweet voice

After years passed in darkness, all changed for that small boy
He grew up, left his home and learned to feel some joy
Neither he nor his mother asked the ogre to come and share
Their brief lives together and sit in the biggest chair

Hidden by the illness, locked behind those doors so strong
Love stayed true, it endured, though the time had been so long
Finally, the past could fade, new realms opened to his view
Memories of the ogre vanished, and his mother was loved anew

Gone

Why do you cry? I gently ask
What can I do? Give me a task
To turn your sadness to a smile
I would run for many a mile

You can't get me what I wish
It cannot be put on any dish
It can't be seen, given as a gift
It is not something you can lift

It isn't a card that you can send
Nor bought if endless pounds to spend
It can't be found in any place
I just want, again, to see her face

No one can tell me, no one knows
But in my mind her memory shows
One day, maybe she will appear
Then I won't shed another tear

Grief

Grief is like a big dark cloud
That covers you all day
And then at night it remains
It will not go away
The colours of the rainbow
Turn to shades of grey
Everything seems different
There is no fun or play

Gradually grief can fade away
The big cloud disappear
And gone will be the anger
The sadness and the fear
You will see the sun can shine
When you forget to wait
Sing and laugh again one day
It will not be too late

I Shall Miss You

I shall miss you when you leave
Your smile and your sweet voice
I shall keep you in my heart
Though you cannot make a noise
I never shall forget our days
The times we spent together
Much laughter amid the tears
In all kinds of weather
Nothing can spoil my memories
No one can dim that view
These are like perennial flowers
Blooming yearly, fresh and new

Life is full of times to share
Some beautiful, some are bad
But all create our inner life
Though sometimes make us sad
Our many special days I keep
In my memory book of you
A smile or tear forever trapped
When my mood is feeling blue
To transport me to happier days
For a while, to a different land
The sun will still be shining
In a place where we can stand

Joyful

I knew a girl
Who had such joy
More than any
Girl or boy

She said it was
Like a light
In her heart
Shining bright

I saw the girl
She had no joy
Less than any
Girl or boy

She said it had
All been taken
And her heart
Was forsaken

I met the girl
And saw her smile
My heart jumped
For a while

She said she had
Got back the light
It had returned
Shining bright

I asked the girl
And she replied
'It was just there
After I cried'

She said that she
Could now play
Sing and dance
Again - all day

Learning To Feel Better

When sadness has eased
And anger is gone
You are left with something
A bit like a song
A song that was made
By that person for you
To help you in life
In all that you do

Something they said
Or a picture is shown
Within your quiet mind
When you are alone
It helps you to know
What you must do
Yes, they can still help
You to get through

They did so before
When in the same place
The difference is now
You can't see the face
You can't feel their arm
Or hear their voice
But just remember
They had no choice

They would want to know
How you are today
But they were taken
And so couldn't stay
Understand and accept
The lesson they gave
Sometimes we must learn
Just to be very brave

Living Without

My dad died, it happened, it was a very awful day
I was told he was too ill and could no longer stay

I miss him, oh so very much, I cried my eyes quite dry
I cannot hold his hand again, no matter how I try

He is not in any room, he never comes through any door
I am getting used to it, it hurts bad, and then some more

If I have something I want to do and I do not know how
I wonder what he would tell me, if he was with me now

I sometimes ask him questions, but I don't know if I'm heard
But I think of the right answer - though he never said a word

He lives with me in memory, there I see his smiling face
If I behave like he did, shall I go to the same place?

I'm told he's gone to heaven - where all good people meet
I have asked, but no one tells me, the name of his new street

When I am old with hair quite grey, I shall not be scared to die
As Dad will be there to greet me, we shall laugh again, not cry

I cannot go until my time. There is not, as yet, a place
But
My Dad will still love me and he'll never forget my face

Loneliness

Surrounded by faces
With laughter around
People so happy
Old friends are found
Amongst the crowd
I want to hear
A familiar voice
But you are not here

The river flows past
A scene of delight
Beauty of mountains
All day and all night
The orchestra plays
Yet I shed a tear
The music is golden
But you are not here

Alone in the quiet
I ask, 'Shall I find
Where you have gone?'
It puzzles my mind
I'm always looking
For somebody dear
And I keep on wishing
That you could be here

Loss

Where has my daddy gone?
Please, can you tell me - now?
I look but I can't find him
And I just don't know how

The last time that I saw him
He hoped to return one day
He didn't want to leave us
But he just couldn't stay

My daddy is an honest man
And to me he would not lie
So why then is he still away?
Does he not really try?

I miss him and I cry so much
I call - he doesn't hear
I know he loved me dearly
So why can't he appear?

If he were dead, would I know?
Or is he lost somewhere?
Is there something I can do?
If not, then I despair.

He may no longer be a part
Of my life - as I grow old
I must live without him
That is what I'm often told

I cannot change anything
Though years will pass away
If he never does come back
My love for him will stay

He will always be my daddy
Wherever he may be
One day perhaps he will know
Just what he meant to me

Lost And Found

When I was little
I had a friend
I used to call her Penny
Someone took her away
And then I hadn't any

When I was tiny
I had a sister
I know her name was Jenny
She was also taken away
Just the same as Penny

As I grew up
I always remembered
Jenny and friend Penny
I searched but I did not find
Them among the many

One day when
I was grown up
I found out who was Penny
But I must wait to look in heaven
To find my sister Jenny

Lost Direction

I saw a man with a smile
He ran beside his boy
Riding a new red bicycle
Two faces - full of joy

I saw the man with a frown
He used a stick to walk
The boy beside him - silent
They could no longer talk

I saw a lonely boy in tears
His father was no more
Death had taken him away
Coffins have no open door

Smoking was the reason
A parent's love became the past
But, the boy had no choice
And grief, for him, would last

No one doubted the father's love
Except the little boy
Angry that he had only been
Second in his father's joy

Memories That Heal

My Grandma died when she was quite old
People live longer these days, we are told
In history gone by few lived a long life
Due to illness, poverty, wars and much strife

I loved my grandma and she loved me too
Anything she asked, I would help her to do
When she died I became dreadfully sad
I cried and I cried, and I felt, oh, so bad

But time had to pass and she couldn't stay
I had to grow up, and must meet every day
So I said goodbye, and remembered her face
And things that we did when I went to her place

The little cooked loaves, made especially for me
Her beautiful garden where she loved to be
In my mind she is there, smiling and pleased
The sadness has melted and my pain has eased

I was lucky to have her, I can hardly explain
What she meant to me, how she helped my pain
Grief followed the going, but once it could heal
That love flows again - now, a warmth I can feel

Missing You Already

I don't like your suitcase
Filled with clothes to wear
It means I cannot see you
That you will not be there
When I wake in the morning
You'll not answer to my call
My birthday will arrive soon
And **you** will miss it all

Each day seems a long time
To me, I am so young
It just isn't the same now
How I wish you hadn't gone
I count days on my fingers
And then use every toe
I hope you will soon be here
I have lots of things to show

But

I shall greet you with a frown
And look away - until at last
My anger all has disappeared
I hope **that** happens fast
So - don't expect a big hug
Or a smile that you can see
Or else you may never know
How much you mean to me

My Dog Died

When my dog was old and ill
The vet couldn't make him better
I said 'Goodbye' and kissed him
Then I wrote my dog a letter
I said I still thought of him
In doggy heaven up above
I sent him my picture thoughts
And lots and lots of love

The vet said in doggy heaven
He'd a friend - who died before
But I asked him if in heaven
Would he walk on a dead floor?
Or would he feel well again?
And romp and play and run?
The vet said that he was sure
He would once again have fun

So I don't mind as I didn't like
To see him in pain and ill
Or see him not eat his food
Or have to take his pill
Or be unable to walk and play
Or even jump or run
So I won't cry any more
And let him have some fun

I think he will understand
He always used to know
If I was sad or I was glad
His tail the truth would show
So I will say 'Goodbye' to him
I can mean that word - at last
And I will buy another dog
My sadness has now passed

My Imaginary World

I wish I could live for ever in
A big house that was round
All the rooms would lead
Into a middle, open ground

We would live in one part
And you could live next door
We could see you as often
And - oh - just so much more

Everyone that we love would
Not be far across the sea
No more long roads to travel
But - all that can never be

Play with friends, go to school
Exciting holidays in the sun
Then - I could talk to you
Tell you everything I'd done

I have read of Round houses
The Vikings built - the same
Why has it all now changed?
I think it's such a shame

I like to have running water
Toilets, warmth and light
But why must you be far away?
For me - that is not right

My Kitten

I used to have a kitten but I haven't. I don't know how
I lost it. Can you help me to try and find it now?
Has anyone seen a kitten? It should be somewhere near
It is ginger coloured with a white stripe by its ear

It has the sweetest little face, its eyes are very blue
If you happen to see it, you will love it too
It is only very tiny, and it isn't very old
It is too young to wander - but can't do what it's told

It is not where I left it, in a basket in the barn
I want it to come back, it belongs **here** at our farm
It had lots of milk to drink and a lovely soft warm bed
It lived with two other cats and a happy life it led

Please don't let it get hurt, wherever it may be
No rat or fox to find it, no nasty dog to see
I thought I saw it yesterday, and I called its name
But when I went to look, that kitten was not the same

Please come back little kitten, you do not need to stray
I shall keep on looking for you - every single day
I only want you to be safe, and loved as you should be
By someone kind and gentle

Oh - how I wish it was still me

My Mum Died

My mum died, she had gone
And left me sad, with no more fun
I could not see her – ever - again
I cried and felt a lot of pain

I lay awake, one night, in bed
And I felt someone stroke my head
I had not heard a voice at all
No one big and no one small

I put on the light so I could see
Who had tried to comfort me
No one was there, but I know
It was my Mum, her love to show

'Just be kind', I was told
Words to remember - until I'm old
'I shall walk with you each day
I had to go, I couldn't stay'

She held my hand - for a while
Tightly, gently, it made me smile
Then she went and took away
My awful pain with her that day

I still miss her, I always will
But I didn't want her to be ill
Though I can never see her face
She visits me in every place

You may feel a mother's love
Shining down from up above
If you are kind and do your best
She will take care of all the rest

No Daddy

I never knew my daddy
He left before I came
My life is fine and I'm OK
But it isn't quite the same
As he is not here for me
To play football in the park
He never reads me stories
Gives no torch when it is dark

Sometimes I wonder - would I see
If he stood by my bed?
But that's just wishful thinking
Only pictures in my head
But I'm sure that he can love
From wherever he may be
And I shall be the kind of boy
To make him proud of me

It was not any of my choice
That he's not here with me
We do not decide these things
What must be is what must be
I have been told that everyone
Has a puzzle they must solve
This is mine, and I know how
To let this one - now - dissolve

I shall stop letting time pass by
Wanting someone I don't know
My anger then can disappear
I shall let **all** the sadness go
I must live my life without him
And do the very best I can
I want to laugh as I grow up
Then I shall be a happy man

One Day

One day I shall be as others
To walk and talk with ease
One day I shall be free of pain
Not troubled with disease
No longer feel restricted
In this body I was given
That would be so amazing
Maybe I dream of heaven

Why was I born with conflict?
In a mind so wild and free
That wants to travel o'er the moors
Up hills, down to the sea?
Yet a body that won't allow
This happiness to be found
I scream - but only in my mind
Silent - I make no sound

There are so many others
Whose lives are very bad
I hear of all their troubles
Their anguish makes me sad
So my own problems fade
When I think of them – not me
The children who are hurting
Are the ones the world should see

But a little anger sometimes felt
A little sadness owned
A little envy - maybe?
But none will there be shown
My life is mine and no one
Can live it my stead
So I will give it 'of my best'
And sleep easy in my bed

Remembering A Dog

Never known to snarl or bite
So gentle all her years
A companion I loved dearly
Her loss caused many tears
She was more than just a friend
A comfort in the storm
When no one else noticed
She has left me - quite forlorn
Yet her passing had to come
It was her time to leave
Watching - while she suffered
Was the worst time of the grief
Will there be another dog
I can love so well?
If I remember with a smile
Then maybe - time will tell

Remembering Grandma

I remember going to see her as often as I could
She lived just down the road - as grandmas really should
Out in her well loved garden, in summer she would be
And always seemed delighted when she caught sight of me

She wasn't very talkative, so, I remember not her voice
She was always very quiet and did not make much noise
She was gentle and so kind, loved me truly, that I know
I used to try to help her - little acts of love I'd show

I used to visit to set her hair and make it look so wavy
She always wore dark coloured clothes, mostly greys or navy
She carried sadness in her heart - from loss of babies - five
Much love, without medicines, could not keep them alive

Yet she was never bitter, never mean or ever cross
A wonderful example, her death was such a loss
I shall remember her kindness as long as I shall live
She never counted a second of the time that she did give

Now, in the spirit world, I am sure she is a queen
A beautiful yellow light - that shines where she has been
Spreading love and happiness, an angel radiant bright
Caring for all children, every day and every night

Sadness Of Loss

I question why I am so sad
I was told your death was near
I sat with you while you left
And did not shed a tear
I was only hoping that you
Had neither pain or fear
I held your hand, just in case
You knew that I was near

Now that you have really gone
It is like a different place
I cannot talk again with you
Nor ever see your face
I only remember you as ill
Weary - too frail to live
After your last illness
You had nothing left to give

I wish I could remember when
You had energy to spare
You were happy as a mother
Who gave me all your care
But at this time a curtain
Has hidden all those years
Maybe the memories will return
When time stops all my tears

Separation

I have a pain
It stays
In my heart

I have a memory
It stays
In my brain

They are linked
The heart and brain
The pain stays

The heart cries
The brain accepts
The pain is eased

Heart and brain
Together forgive
But do not forget

Someone Has Left

We used to play 'Happy Families'
But now it is too hard
As in our family we are missing
A very special card

It wasn't lost, or even torn
It just went, and it was gone
We are feeling very sad
And our game is not much fun

Someone might find it for us
Put it back into our pack
We are becoming quite prepared
For it never coming back

You can't play 'Happy Families'
When one has gone astray
We'll have to play another game
And put this one away

The Child's Dog

The child and dog had gone out to play
In the nearby field, like a normal day
She was a spaniel, her hair was golden
The child's heart was to her beholden

A loving companion for the child
A dog with nature - meek and mild
A cross word was never spoken
But one day, her heart was broken

A gamekeeper wanted rid of foxes
Took poisoned food out of his boxes
And put it in the nearby wood
To the poor dog it just tasted good

But disaster struck, no one knew why
It was that small dog's time to die
The child thought 'I am to blame'
Though that was never the adult's aim

A dog does not know what is best
Will eat what's there, it does not test
Scavenging is their way of life
Adults please watch - to lessen strife

Grief struck deep into her heart
It took away a special part
She had to learn to be quite strong
To remember good times all life long

The feeling of a warmth that stayed
On her leg where the dog had laid
The comfort of its gentle touch
And why she loved her dog so much

The Jigsaw

Something is missing
The jigsaw is complete
I see the finished picture
Clearly, very sweet
A child sitting on the floor
Alone, she quietly thinks
Her dress is light blue with
Flowers in different pinks
She is not smiling
Yet, no tears can I see
Something is missing
Whatever can it be?

Something is missing
But what? I do not know
Is it the isolation
The picture seems to show?
No dolls, no books
Nothing to be found
A picture of loneliness
A child sat on the ground
No one can explain and
No clue can I see
Something is missing
Whatever can it be?

Something was missing
The answer I now know
The child sitting by herself
Silent grief did show
Her dearest friend was gone
Suddenly had been taken
She would never hear her
She felt quite forsaken
In her life she had been
But someone closed a door
Something was missing
She would see her face no more

Time Passes

I stand by the window
I sit by the door
But he never calls
My name anymore

I walk in the town
I walk down the street
But he's never there
For me to meet

I lay in bed thinking
I wait in my chair
But he never arrives
It just isn't fair

I must just be brave
I must understand
That he will never
Again hold my hand

A short time is better
Than no time at all
He taught me to care
When I was just small

He taught me to be sad
When he went away
But sadness can pass
It will do, one day

But I will grow up
And never forget
He always loved me
I'm so glad that we met

Was It Necessary

I keep a piece of paper
The last letter he did write
It is written in black ink
On paper that is white

I wrote a letter back
Which I know he never read
It was returned to our mother
And this is what it said

'Your son died in a battle
His life was not in vain
He was badly wounded but
He did not die in pain'

I keep that piece of paper
My brother sent to me
He will never come back home
His face I shall not see

If all men had to feel my pain
They would **never, ever** fight
And I would not have to cry
Myself to sleep at night

What Went Wrong

I can see an empty chair
In silent room – a vacant bed
His posters are upon the wall
Now, **we** look at them - instead

His bike waits in the garage
There is no one on the seat
It was his pride and his joy
But, again - we shall not meet

What madness possessed him?
He was sensible and kind
What changed his personality?
What got into his mind?

The drug that he was given
He had no need to take
With stupidity or in weakness
He made his last mistake

Others are left with sadness
Some cry and some are mad
But nothing can bring back to us
The friend that we once had

<u>Why</u>

My brother died
I am so mad
He took drugs
He wasn't bad
He paid the price
Now he has gone
No way back
The damage done

My brother died
I am so sad
He took drugs
He wasn't bad
But someone else
Gave him a pill
They are alive
They did kill

My brother died
Short life he had
He took drugs
He wasn't bad
He was loved
We ask 'Why?'
No one knows
And I just cry

You Died

You died, I have an empty place
The sadness shows upon my face
But I can see you in my mind
In memories you left behind

When you took me out to play
In the park that snowy day
We ran around, we had great fun
Now I know those times are gone

The day we visited the zoo
There was still so much more to do
But rain came down - just like a sheet
And we got wet from head to feet

I am told you've gone to heaven
I don't know - I'm only seven
But, in my mind a picture keep
To look at when I go to sleep

You are smiling, like that day
Before the one you went away
Do you remember the sea and sand?
We paddled, I still feel your hand

You didn't tell me you would die
Didn't you want to see me cry?
Or was it that you didn't know?
Or why our walk was very slow?

But, just for now, I cannot smile
It seems to be a long, long while
Till I can see you once again
And I have got an awful pain

I will be happy again one day
I shall laugh and I shall play
Or else I think you will be sad
I want my life to make you glad

A different message